A Crabtree Branches Book

Let's Go Fish

PIER FISHING

By Kerri Mazzarella

T0020661

CRABTREE
Publishing Company
www.crabtreebooks.com

School-to-Home Support for Caregivers and Teachers

This high-interest book is designed to motivate striving students with engaging topics while building fluency, vocabulary, and an interest in reading. Here are a few questions and activities to help the reader build upon his or her comprehension skills.

Before Reading:
- *What do I think this book is about?*
- *What do I know about this topic?*
- *What do I want to learn about this topic?*
- *Why am I reading this book?*

During Reading:
- *I wonder why...*
- *I'm curious to know...*
- *How is this like something I already know?*
- *What have I learned so far?*

After Reading:
- *What was the author trying to teach me?*
- *What are some details?*
- *How did the photographs and captions help me understand more?*
- *Read the book again and look for the vocabulary words.*
- *What questions do I still have?*

Extension Activities:
- *What was your favorite part of the book? Write a paragraph on it.*
- *Draw a picture of your favorite thing you learned from the book.*

TABLE OF CONTENTS

WHERE TO FISH

Pier fishing is a type of saltwater fishing that takes place on a pier. It is a great way to catch saltwater fish without going on a boat.

There are piers located all around North America. A fishing pier, also known as a **jetty**, can be very exciting for anglers of any age.

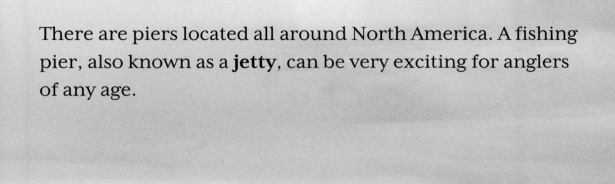

FUN FACTS

The Ocean View Pier and Restaurant, located in Norfolk, Virginia, is the longest freestanding fishing pier in North America.

Knowing where to fish on the pier is important. Bigger fish are found toward the end of the dock in deeper water.

Watching birds can help you choose the spot to fish.
When they are flying and circling in a certain area,
you can bet fish are there!

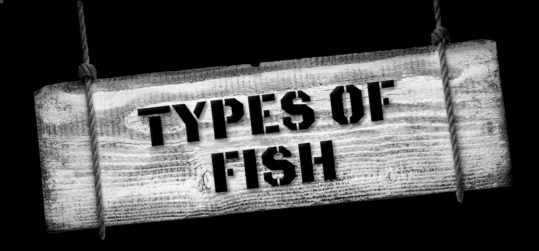

TYPES OF FISH

Many species of saltwater fish are caught pier fishing. Some are large and some are small. The possibilities of what you can catch are endless!

sheepshead

flounder

Flounder, sheepshead, snapper, redfish, black drum, and grouper are excellent fish to catch from a pier. They are very tasty to eat.

Tarpon, cobia, and mackerel are fish that are bigger in size and considered a prize catch. Sometimes sharks are caught off the pier.

baby shark

king mackerel

The **king mackerel**, also known as a king fish, is a great catch. Many people like to smoke this fish and make fish dip.

SAFETY AND RULES

Unlike other types of fishing, most states in the US allow you to fish from a pier without a **fishing license**. Other piers may require you to pay an entrance fee or fishing fee or even both.

Some piers open and close at certain times. Be sure to check times before heading to fish. Not all piers will have time restrictions.

FUN FACTS

Fish like to hang around piers. Drop your line right by the pier. No casting required.

red drum

It is important to know size limitations and seasons
for types of fish you are planning to catch. Certain fish
cannot be kept if they are over or under a specific size.

Fishing piers can sometimes be busy and crowded. Be sure to give fellow anglers enough room to cast and fish. Hook injuries are common so be cautious when casting your line.

RODS AND EQUIPMENT

OC FISHING PIER
ICE
GIFTS
ROD RENTAL
BAIT AND TACKLE
SNACKS AND COLD DRINKS

ICE

Special equipment is used for pier fishing. There are several spinning rod and reel combinations to choose from. They can be purchased separately or together.

Some fishing piers have equipment rental stations. You can rent a fishing rod combo instead of buying one.

FUN FACTS

Fish like to hide. Anglers sometimes sink objects by piers to create hiding places, then return later to fish there.

For beginners it is best to start with a rod and reel combo. The type of fish you are trying to catch will determine the size of the rod, reel, and line.

The average rod and reel saltwater combo can be purchased for around $80.

Some other equipment to bring are a bucket for your catch, a net, a **gaff**, and a chair.

It is a long distance from the water to the top of the pier. A gaff can help you secure your catch when you have a fish on your line.

19

WHAT'S IN YOUR TACKLE BOX?

It is a good idea to bring a **tackle box** when pier fishing. You never know what you might need. A big fish could snap your line taking your weight, hook, and **bait**!

Your tackle box should contain extra line, hooks, weights, **sinkers**, and lures. Sinkers are important to bring your bait down to the bottom of the water.

sinker

You can purchase a beginner saltwater tackle box for around $60.

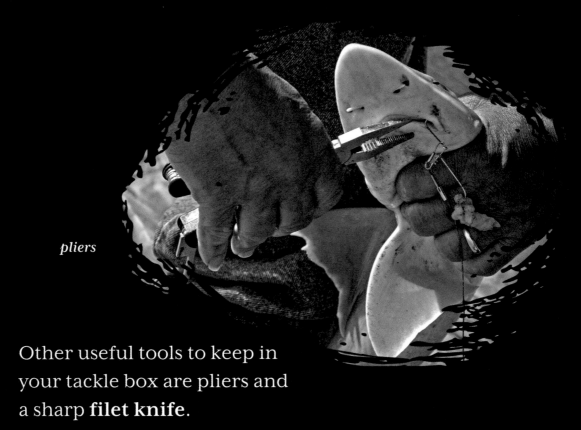

pliers

Other useful tools to keep in your tackle box are pliers and a sharp **filet knife**.

filet knife

A good set of pliers costs around $15 and a filet knife is around $20.

Most anglers build their tackle box little by little. It is fun to add new items to your tackle box as you learn more about pier fishing.

TYPES OF BAIT

What bait you choose to use is up to you. The options are endless. Your location can help you decide which bait to choose. Some piers will have a bait shop.

saltwater lures

Both live bait and artificial bait are great choices for pier fishing. The good thing about live bait is that you can save money by catching it yourself with a **sabiki rig**. Lures are an artificial bait that come in all shapes, colors, and sizes.

Popular bait for pier fishing includes shrimp, squid, sardines, blood worms, sand fleas, and anchovies.

shrimp

squid

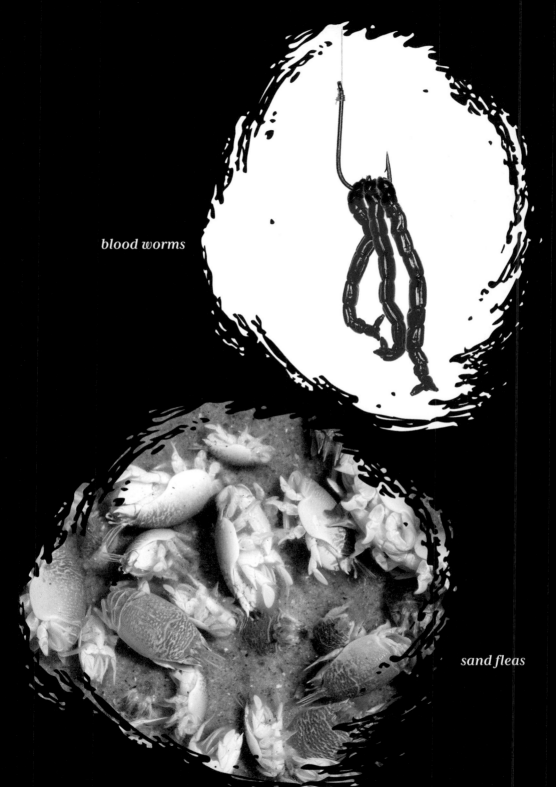

blood worms

sand fleas

Pier fishing is a fun hobby that can be done any time of the year. Both young and old anglers enjoy this type of fishing. Seek out the closest pier, drop a line, and get hooked on fishing.

GLOSSARY

bait (beyt): Food used to entice fish or other animals as prey

filet knife (fi-LEY nahyf): A sharp knife used to cut and prepare fish

fishing license (FISH-ing LAHY-suhns): A legal document allowing a person to fish

flounder (FLOUN-der): A flatfish; type of fish that has a flat body and is often eaten as food

gaff (gaf): A spear or hook used for lifting heavy fish

jetty (JET-ee): A structure or pier built out onto the water to influence the current or protect a harbor

king mackerel (king MAK-er-uhl): A migratory species of fish located in the western Atlantic Ocean that is noted as a fighting sportfish

pier fishing (peer FISH-ing): A type of fishing that takes place on a pier or jetty

sabiki rig (sa-BEE-kee rig): Typically used off piers or boats, line consisting of 6-10 tiny hooks, used to catch small fish

sinker (SING-ker): A special weight used to sink a fishing line

tackle box (TAK-uhl boks): A box designed for fishing equipment